Primary Partners®
Singing Fun!

I Belong to The Church of Jesus Christ of Latter-day Saints

• Learning Activities and Awards to Motivate Singing Fun!
• Pictures to Teach Songs   • Songs Coordinate with Sharing Time Themes
• Use for Sharing Time and Family Home Evening

Introducing the Author and Illustrator, Creators of the Following Series of Books and CD-ROMS:

Primary Partners® manual match activities, Sharing Time, Singing Fun, and Achievement Days, *Young Women Fun-tastic! Activities for Manuals 1-3 and Personal Progress Motivators*, *Gospel Fun Activities*, *Super Singing Activities*, *Super Little Singers*, *File Folder Family Home Evenings*, and *Home-spun Fun Family Home Evenings*

Mary Ross, Author

Mary Ross is an energetic mother, and has been a Primary teacher, and Achievement Days leader. She loves to help children and young women have a good time while learning. She has studied acting, modeling, and voice. Her varied interests include writing, creating activities and children's parties, and cooking. Mary and her husband, Paul, live with their daughter, Jennifer, in Sandy, Utah.

Jennette Guymon-King, Illustrator

Jennette Guymon-King has studied graphic arts and illustration at Utah Valley College and the University of Utah. She served a mission to Japan. Jennette enjoys sports, reading, cooking, art, gardening, and freelance illustrating. Jennette and her husband Clayton, live in Riverton, Utah. They are the proud parents of their daughter Kayla Mae, and sons Levi and Carson.

Copyright © 2002 by Mary H. Ross and Jennette Guymon-King
All Rights Reserved

Covenant Communications, Inc.
American Fork, Utah

Printed in Canada
First Printing: December 2002

Primary Partners® *Singing Fun!: I Belong to The Church of Jesus Christ of Latter-day Saints*
ISBN 1-59156-141-8

ACKNOWLEDGMENTS: Thanks to Inspire Graphics (www.inspiregraphics.com) for the use of Lettering Delights computer fonts. —This product is neither sponsored nor endorsed by The Church of Jesus Christ of Latter-day Saints.

INTRODUCTION
Primary Partners—Singing Time Fun!

Teaching children to sing is easy with this volume of visuals, activities, and awards. In just minutes children can learn to sing these songs that coordinate with the 2003 sharing time theme:
"I Belong to The Church of Jesus Christ of Latter-day Saints."

This book may be used in both Primary and family home evening to help children learn to appreciate why they belong to the Church and to realize that through the gospel of Jesus Christ they can obtain eternal life, life with Heavenly Father and Jesus. The songs will help children desire to live the commandments and honor Jesus Christ through honoring their baptismal covenants. These songs will increase children's knowledge that they are children of God and look forward to being a part of God's kingdom on earth and in heaven.

> VISUALS AVAILABLE IN COLOR: These *Singing Fun* illustrations are available on CD-ROM ready to print in color or black and white (shown on the back cover).

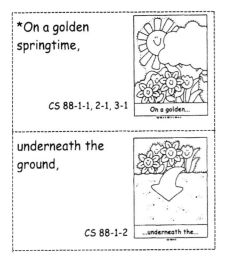

*On a golden springtime,

CS 88-1-1, 2-1, 3-1

On a golden...

underneath the ground,

CS 88-1-2   ...underneath the...

HOW TO USE SONGS AND VISUALS:

USING STARTER WORDS AND CODES:

Even Junior Primary children will feel confident as they sing along when you use these learning visuals. Those who can't read can view the pictures. For those who can read, on some songs, there are starter words to lead children into each verse. Example, in Song 2, "On a Golden Springtime" the phrase *"On a golden . . ."* leads them into the next word (or phrase) . . . *"springtime"* (shown below/left).

Cut out and mount the cue cards (sample shown left) on the back of each matching visual. The cards show the page number, verse, and visual number of each visual, to keep them in sequential order. See "How to Read the Codes" below. This will help the singing leader, parent, or older children know the words for each visual they are holding for the others to see.

How to Read the Codes:

- Song 2, example shown above reads: CS 88-1-2. This means *Children's Songbook*, page 88, verse 1, visual 1. The next code CS 88-1-2 is verse 1, visual 2. If more numbers follow (as shown above), they indicate the visual is to be shown a second and third time at the beginning of each verse.
- On the song(s) that have a chorus you will find a "C" after the page number, e.g., CS 2-C-1 on page 24.

ANOTHER WAY TO SHOW VISUALS:

Cut out the visual (example shown right), cutting on the dotted lines, leaving off the background portions and words to mount on an object, e.g., a straw or a wooden craft stick.

he prophecies of long...

CS 88-1-1

WAYS TO SHOW VISUALS:

You can display the visuals in different ways to create variety, interest, and participation. We suggest that all visuals be laminated for durability. Here are some fun ways to present the visuals:

• **PLACE ON STRAWS OR STICKS** (shown left and on the previous page): Tape a straw, or tongue depressor, or popsicle stick to the back of each visual as a holder. When doing this, make sure the coding cue cards (words and code numbers) are glued to the top back of each visual. Children may be chosen to come to the front and hold the visuals as the Primary sings the song. This method is best when using ONLY the picture (cutting out the background and words), as the 8 ½" x 11" sheet is too large and will be floppy unless reinforced.

• **POSTERS** (shown right): Display the visuals on a poster or cardboard. As you teach the song, and as children appear ready, remove a few of the visuals to test their memory, or mix up the order of the visuals.

Savior, may I lea...

Walk the path that...

Pause to help...

Finding strength...

• **STRING OF PICTURES** (shown left): Use visuals to choose songs to sing. Put one visual from each song in a bag and have a child draw from the bag. Children can try to guess the song from the visual and then sing it.

• **HIDE VISUALS:**
1. Tape visual to the bottom of children's chair or hidden in the room. Ask one class at a time to find the hidden visual(s).
2. Children can help you hide the visuals. When the child comes back in, children can say, "warm, warmer, hot" as the seeker gets closer to the visual, or "cold, colder, freezing" as he or she gets further away from the visual.

Activities to Motivate Singing Fun!

Necktie Singing Meter:

Ahead of time, provide the bishop with an old tie to wear as he visits singing time. Tell children that depending on how well they sing, they can cut an inch or more off the bishop's tie. Children really get involved and sing well for this activity. Cut the tie clear up to the knot. Then, in front of the children, ask the bishop to wear the tie to the rest of the meetings, telling others how well the children sang.

Seasonal or Anytime Motivators:

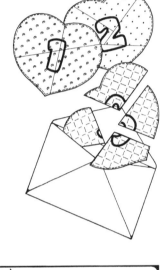

1. "Sing with All Your Heart" Pick-a-Song:

Children will be motivated to sing when they can put together a puzzle to know which song to sing.

To Make: *Copy, color, and cut out the 1-12 heart puzzles (pages 96-99). Laminate and cut into puzzle pieces, placing each individual puzzle in an envelope.

To Use: Ahead of time hide the 12 puzzle envelopes in the room, and write the numbers 1-12 on the board with a song and page by each number, e.g., write 1. I Am a Child of God, page 2. To save time, write the 1-12 songs on a poster and mount the poster on the board when ready to sing. Sing as many songs as you can, choosing children one at a time to find a puzzle and put it together to pick a song.

Note: The leader who knows where the puzzles are can say, "warm, warmer, hot" as the seeker gets closer, or "cold, colder, freezing" as he or she gets farther away from the puzzle.

2. "Egg"-stra Special Singers! Pick-a-Song:

Use this activity to help children choose songs and sing in a different way by choosing a chick hidden in the basket.

To Make: *Copy, color, and cut out the basket parts A and B, and two or three sets of eggs and chicks (pages 100-102). Mount the basket on a poster and laminate the entire poster. Laminate the eggs and chicks. Write the names of the songs the children are familiar with and the ones they are practicing on the back of the eggs. Write ways children can sing on the backs of chick, e.g., softer, louder, sing standing up, sing with arms folded, sing with eyes closed, sing turned around, only boys sing, only girls sing, sing with a big smile. Mount the eggs in the basket with tape, and hide the chick behind the eggs.

You're "Egg"stra Special Singers!

To Use: Ask children to come up and choose an egg. Sing the song on the back of the egg chosen. If a child finds a chick behind the egg, ask children to sing the way the chick suggests, e.g., eyes closed.

"Bee"utiful Singing!

Some leaves may tangle, but they can still dance.

3. "Bee"-utiful Singing Flowers! Meter:

Children can be encouraged to sing songs better as you mount these "Needs Practice," "Great Improvement!," and "Bloomin' Spectacular!" flowers, one on top of the other.

To Make: *Copy, color, and cut out the flowers and several sets of bees (pages 103-106). Write practice song titles on the front of each bee before laminating images. You may need extra bees (leaving them blank) to use for other songs or to use simply as a marker (detailed below). You will need a light blue poster to mount the visuals. Mount the flowers as shown left on the poster and then laminate this entire poster for durability.

To Use: Use the bees as markers to place next to the flowers after singing each song, e.g, if you sing "The Things I Do" song and they don't do as well as you would like, post the bee with that song title on the "Needs Practice" flower. Then next week you can see where the song ended up on the chart and practice so that bee can get up to the higher flowers. You can add song titles to the blank bees, or simply use one bee as a marker for judging one song and rating the song after the song is sung.

4. Dancing Leaves Pick-a-Song:

Mount leaves on a fan so children can see them blowing as they grab a leaf to pick-a-song.

To Make: *Copy, color, and cut out the leaves (page 107) making as many as you need for the songs. Write on the back of each leaf the children's favorite songs and songs they are practicing. Attach a 6-inch curling ribbon on each leaf and tie each to the front of a large fan. Place them far apart so they don't tangle easily. By using curling ribbon to attach the leaves to the fan, you can curl the end of the ribbon making it easy to thread through the screen bars. Tie ribbon to the fan.

To Use: Tell children they can pick-a-song by catching a dancing leaf. Turn on the fan and have children come up one at a time to grab a dancing leaf. Hold onto the fan so the children don't pull it over. After each choice, turn off the fan and cut the ribbon close to the leaf to release the leaf.

*All of the images can be printed in color or black and white using the *Primary Partners Singing Fun!*
I Belong to The Church of Jesus Christ of Latter-day Saints CD-ROM.

5. Scarecrow Sing-a-long Meter:

Children can build a scarecrow or hide the corn behind the crows to keep them interested in singing.

To Make: *Copy, color, and cut out the scarecrow parts and several crows and corn (pages 108-113). Write the titles of practice songs or children's favorite songs on the back of the crows. Write ways children can sing the songs on the back of the corn, e.g., boys only, girls only, softer, louder, hum, faster, slower, or actions, e.g., eyes closed, hands on ears, flap arm/wings like a crow (putting hands under arms and flapping elbows).

To Use:

Option 1—Build a Scarecrow: Arrange the scarecrow pieces randomly along the side of a poster or board, or put the pieces in a bag to draw from. When a piece is chosen, the child or leader can read the song and the child can tape the piece to the poster or board to build the scarecrow. Children can choose the pieces in any order, e.g., they can choose a head before they choose a leg. Have them position it about where it will end up.

Option 2—Pick a Song and Ways to Sing: Put the scarecrow together and post the crows along the arms, on the hat, or on the ground next to the flowers. Post the corn cobs behind the crows. Have children take turns choosing a crow to determine the song to sing. If they uncover a crow and find the corn, read the back of the corn to learn how they should sing the song, e.g., boys only.

6. Super Singer Awards and Happy Birthday Buttons:

Children will feel like singing better than ever with these Super Singer awards. They will feel special when it's their birthday if they can wear a Happy Birthday button.

To Make: *Copy, color, and cut out awards and buttons (pages 114-119). Laminate for durability. Awards and buttons can be pinned on the child with a small safety pin, or roll a piece of tape, and tape to the child's clothes.

To Use:

Super Singer Awards: There are two ways the awards can be given:

1. When using the 1-5 seasonal activities (previously shown here), e.g., the Scarecrow Pick-a-song, give out the "You're singing is music to my ear!" corncob singing award.

2. Or, place a mixture of all the awards in a container for children to draw from anytime children are singing well.

Happy Birthday Buttons: When you sing happy birthday to a child, award them with a Happy Birthday button.

*All of the images can be printed in color or black and white using the *Primary Partners Singing Fun!* *I Belong to The Church of Jesus Christ of Latter-day Saints* CD-ROM.

TABLE OF CONTENTS
Primary Partners Singing Time Fun!

I Belong to The Church of Jesus Christ of Latter-day Saints

Songs and Visuals That Coordinate with the 2003 Sharing Time Themes:

Activities to Motivate Singing Fun!
(See Introduction for Details)

Theme 2 Song "On a Golden Springtime"   *Children's Songbook—page 88*

Note: Copy the "On a golden springtime" CS 88-1-1, 2-1, 3-1 visual and cue card three times and mount the cue card on the back. Or, show the one visual at the beginning of each verse.

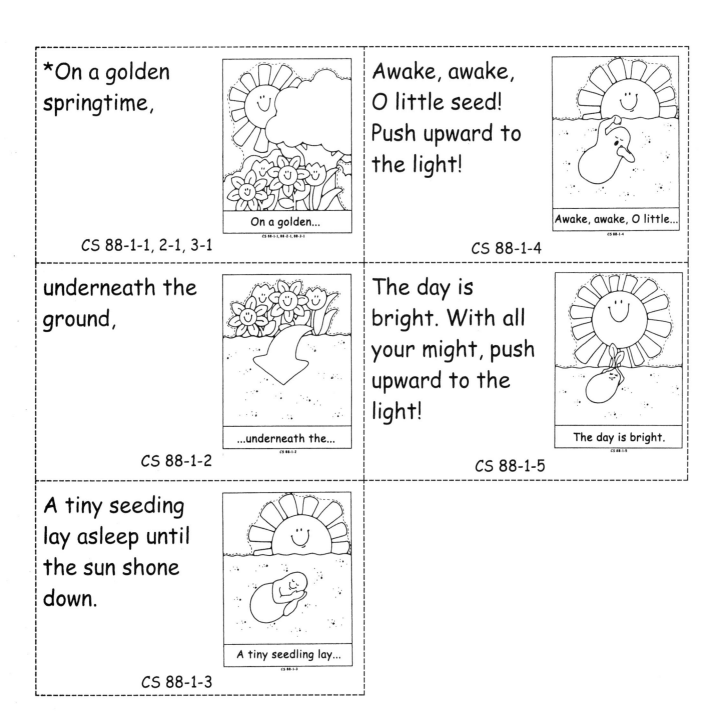

*On a golden springtime,

On a golden...

CS 88-1-1, 2-1, 3-1

underneath the ground,

...underneath the...

CS 88-1-2

A tiny seeding lay asleep until the sun shone down.

A tiny seedling lay...

CS 88-1-3

Awake, awake, O little seed! Push upward to the light!

Awake, awake, O little...

CS 88-1-4

The day is bright. With all your might, push upward to the light!

The day is bright.

CS 88-1-5

Page 1 (pages 3-15 visuals follow) "On a Golden Springtime," *Children's Songbook*, page 88,
Words: Virginia Maughan Kammeyer, 1925-1999. © 1989 IRI
Music: Crawford Gates, b. 1921. © 1989 IRI

Theme 2 Song "On a Golden Springtime"   *Children's Songbook—page 88*

Jesus Christ
awoke

CS 88-2-2   ...Jesus Christ awoke

CS 88-2-2

in a forest
glade,

CS 88-3-2   ...in a forest glade,...

CS 88-3-2

And left the
tomb where he
had lain; the
bands of death
he broke.

And left the tomb...

CS 88-2-3

CS 88-2-3

The Father and
the Son
appeared as
Joseph knelt
and prayed.

The Father and the...

CS 88-3-3

CS 88-3-3

Awake, awake,
O sleeping world!
Look upward to
the light,

CS 88-2-4   Awake, awake, O...

CS 88-2-4

Awake, awake, O
nations all!
Receive the
gospel light!

CS 88-3-4   Awake, awake, O...

CS 88-3-4

For now all men
may live again.
Look upward to
the light!

CS 88-2-5   For now all men may...

CS 88-2-5

The gospel true
is here for you.
Receive its
glorious light!

The gospel true is...

CS 88-3-5

CS 88-3-5

Page 2 (pages 3-15 visuals follow) "On a Golden Springtime," *Children's Songbook*, page 88,
Words: Virginia Maughan Kammeyer, 1925-1999. © 1989 IRI
Music: Crawford Gates, b. 1921. © 1989 IRI

On a golden...

...underneath the...

A tiny seedling lay...

Awake, awake, O little...

The day is bright.

...Jesus Christ awoke

CS 88-2-2

And left the tomb...

Awake, awake, O...

For now all men may...

...in a forest glade,...

The Father and the...

Awake, awake, O...

The gospel true is...

Theme 3 Song "I Am a Child of God"   *Children's Songbook—pages 2-3*
You May Want to Use the Following Visuals with the Song:

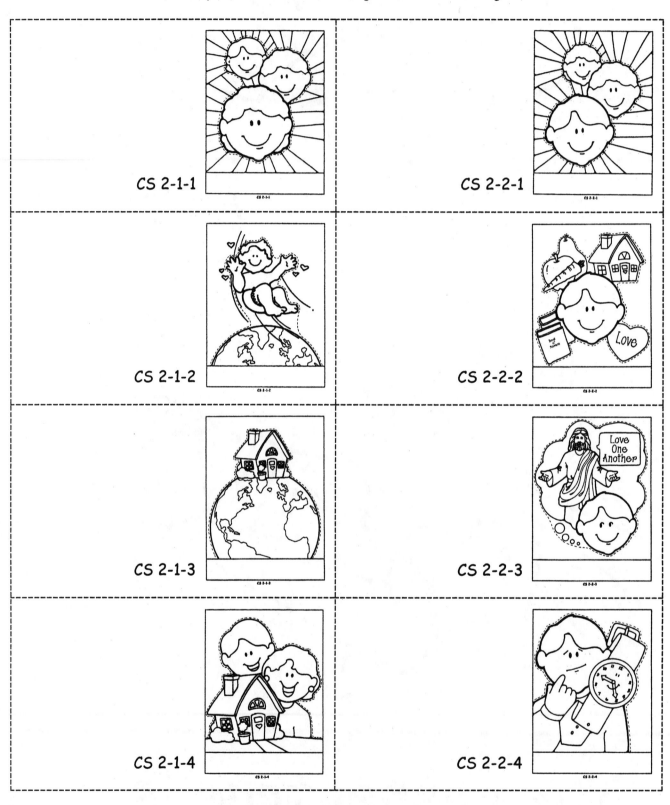

CS 2-1-1

CS 2-2-1

CS 2-1-2

CS 2-2-2

CS 2-1-3

CS 2-2-3

CS 2-1-4

CS 2-2-4

Theme 3 Song "I Am a Child of God"   *Children's Songbook*—pages 2-3

You May Want to Use the Following Visuals with the Song:

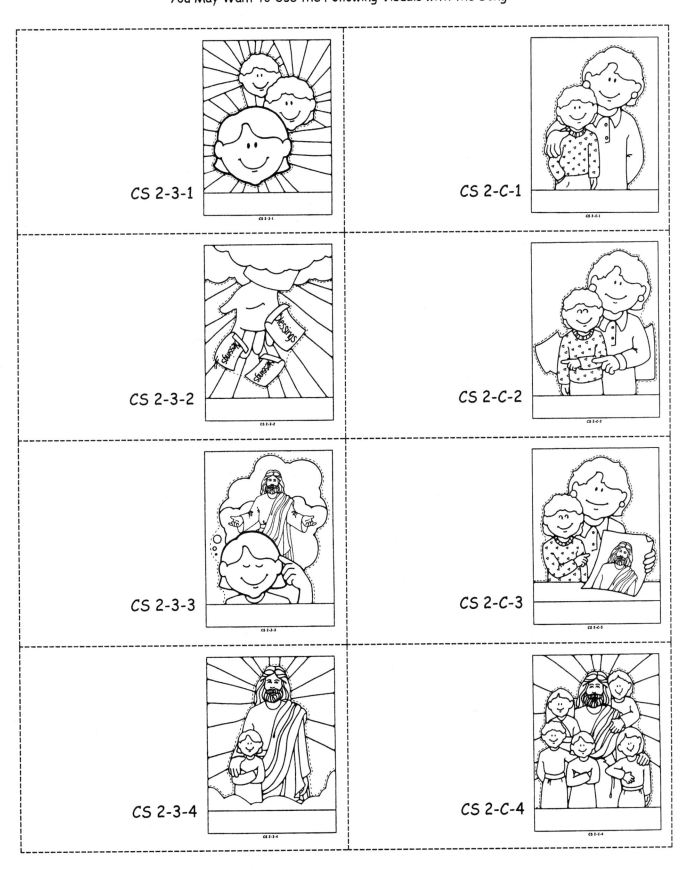

CS 2-1-1

CS 2-1-2

CS 2-1-3

CS 2-1-4

CS 2-2-1

Book
of
Mormon

Love

CS 2-2-4

CS 2-3-1

CS 2-3-2

CS 2-3-4

CS 2-C-1

CS 2-C-2

Theme 4 Song "Easter Hosanna"   *Children's Songbook—pages 68-69*

The prophecies of long ago now at last fulfilled,

CS 68-1-1

When Jesus Christ appeared to Nephites in the promised land,

CS 68-2-1

When Jesus risen from the dead, to man Himself revealed.

CS 68-1-2

The righteous people saw his wounds and came to understand

CS 68-2-2

As he came down from heav'n above, white robed and glorified,

CS 68-1-3

That he, once dead, was risen up as Savior, Lord and King.

CS 68-2-3

The people of the promised land received their Lord and cried:

CS 68-1-4

As they rejoiced, now we rejoice, and joyfully sing;

CS 68-2-4

Page 34 (pages 35-43 visuals follow)

"Easter Hosanna," *Children's Songbook*, pages 68-69, Words and Music: Vanja Y. Watkins, b. 1938. © 1982 IRI

Hosanna! Blessed be the name of the Most High God!
(repeat)

CS 68-C-1

The prophecies of long...

When Jesus risen...

CS 68-1-2

As he came down from...

The people of the....

When Jesus Christ...

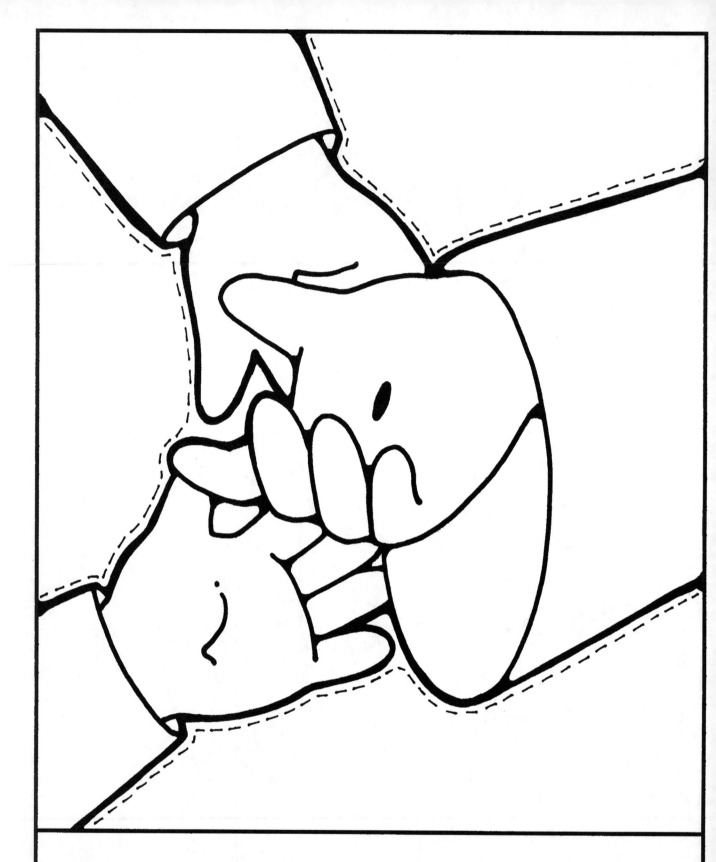

The righteous people...

That he, once dead...

As they rejoiced, now...

Hosanna! Blessed be...

Theme 5 Song "The Things I Do"   *Children's Songbook—pages 170-171*

I'm much too young to go abroad To teach and preach the word of God,

CS 170-1-1

I'm much too young to...

CS 170-1-1

I'll take my friend to church with me, where I will act with dignity.

CS 170-3-1

I'll take my friend to...

CS 170-3-1

But I can show I know it's true, Quite simply, by the things I do.

CS 170-1-2

But I can show I know...

CS 170-1-2

My reverence and my happy face Will tell him it's a sacred place.

CS 170-3-2

My reverence and my...

CS 170-3-2

The people in my neighborhood Will judge the gospel bad or good

CS 170-2-1

The people in my...

CS 170-2-1

In everything I do he'll see I am what I profess to be.

CS 170-4-1

In everything I do...

CS 170-4-1

By how I act at work and play, And not just on the Sabbath day.

CS 170-2-2

But how I act at work...

CS 170-2-2

Then when the elders find his door, He'll say, "Come in and tell me more."

CS 170-4-2

Then when the elders...

CS 170-4-2

Page 44 (pages 45-52 visuals follow) "The Things I Do," *Children's Songbook*, pages 170-171, Words and Music: L. Clair Likes, 1908-1998. © 1975 IRI
Music: Vanja Y. Watking, b. 1938. © 1975 IRI

I'm much too young to...

But I can show I know...

The people in my...

But how I act at work...

I'll take my friend to...

My reverence and my...

In everything I do...

Then when the elders...

Theme 6 Song "I Lived in Heaven"   *Children's Songbook—page 4*

I lived in heaven a long time ago, it is true;

CS 4-1-1

Father said he needed someone who had enough love

CS 4-2-1

Lived there and loved there with people I know. So did you.

CS 4-1-2

To give his life so we all can return there above.

CS 4-2-2

Then Heavenly Father presented a beautiful plan,

CS 4-1-3

There was another who sought for the honor divine.

CS 4-2-3

All about earth and eternal salvation for man.

CS 4-1-4

Jesus said, "Father, send me, and the glory be thine."

CS 4-2-4

Theme 6 Song "I Lived in Heaven"   *Children's Songbook—page 4*

Jesus was chosen, and as the Messiah he came,

CS 4-3-1

Jesus was chosen...

CS 4-3-1

Conquering evil and death through his glorious name,

CS 4-3-2

Conquering evil and...

CS 4-3-2

Giving us hope of a wonderful life yet to be

CS 4-3-3

Giving us hope of a...

CS 4-3-3

Home in that heaven where Father is waiting for me.

CS 4-3-4

Home in that heaven...

CS 4-3-4

Page 54 (pages 55-66 visuals follow)   "I Lived in Heaven," *Children's Songbook*, page 4,
Words and Music: Janeen Jacobs Brady, b. 1934. © 1987 by Janeen Jacobs Brady.
This song may be copied for incidental, noncommercial church or home use.

I lived in heaven a...

Lived there and loved...

Then Heavenly Father...

All about earth and...

Father said he needed...

To give his life so we...

There was another...

Jesus said, "Father,...

CS 4-2-4

Jesus was chosen...

CS 4-3-1

Conquering evil and...

Giving us hope of a...

Home in that heaven...

Theme 7 Song "Lord, I Would Follow Thee"   *Hymns*—page 220

You May Want to Use the Following Visuals with the Song:

NOTE: When teaching this song, tell children that the last line is the same for every verse and the second to the last line is the same as the first line. Then follow with the last line.

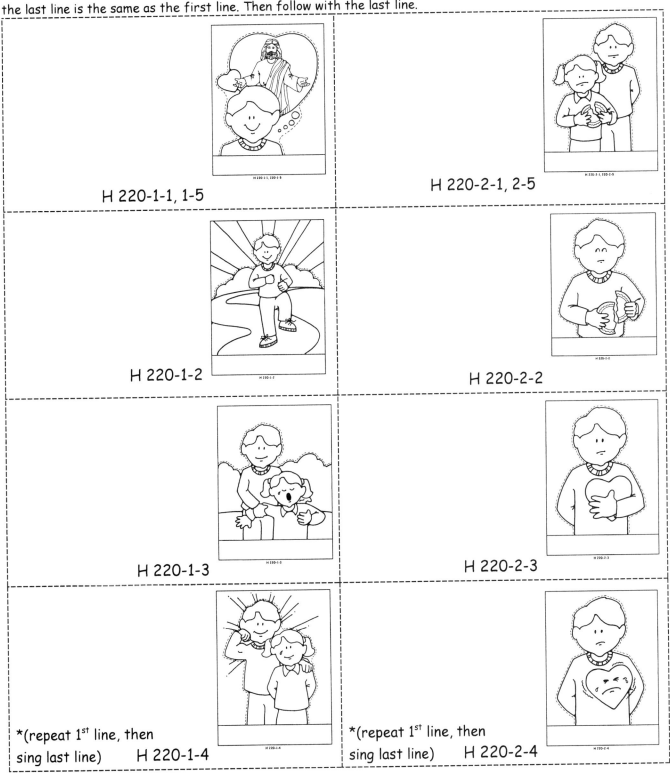

H 220-1-1, 1-5

H 220-2-1, 2-5

H 220-1-2

H 220-2-2

H 220-1-3

H 220-2-3

*(repeat 1st line, then sing last line)   H 220-1-4

*(repeat 1st line, then sing last line)   H 220-2-4

Page 67 (pages 69-84 visuals follow)

Theme 7 Song "Lord, I Would Follow Thee"   *Hymns*—page 220

You May Want to Use the Following Visuals with the Song:

NOTE: When teaching this song, tell children that the last line is the same for every verse and the second to the last line is the same as the first line. Then follow with the last line.

H 220-3-1, 3-5

H 220-4-1, 4-5

H 220-3-2

H 220-4-2

H 220-3-3

H 220-4-3

*(repeat 1st line, then sing last line)   H 220-3-4

*(repeat 1st line, then sing last line)   H 220-4-4

Page 68 (pages 69-84 visuals follow)

H 220-1-2

H 220-1-3

H 220-1-4

H 220-2-3

H 220-3-1, 220-3-5

H 220-3-4

H 220-4-4

Theme 8 Song "Choose the Right Way"   *Children's Songbook—pages 160-161*
You May Want to Use the Following Visuals with the Song:

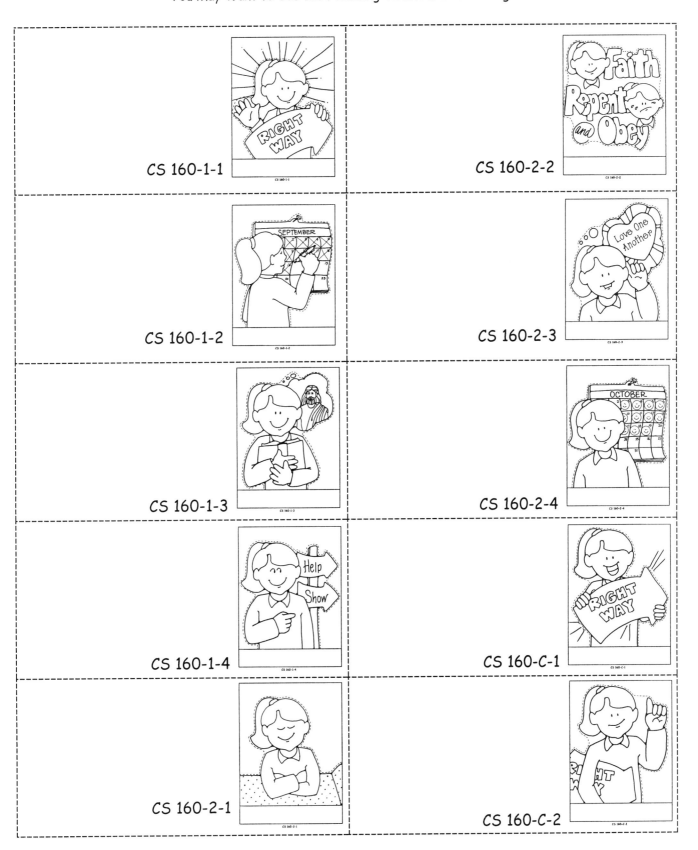

CS 160-1-1

CS 160-2-2

CS 160-1-2

CS 160-2-3

CS 160-1-3

CS 160-2-4

CS 160-1-4

CS 160-C-1

CS 160-2-1

CS 160-C-2

CS 160-2-1

CS 160-C-2

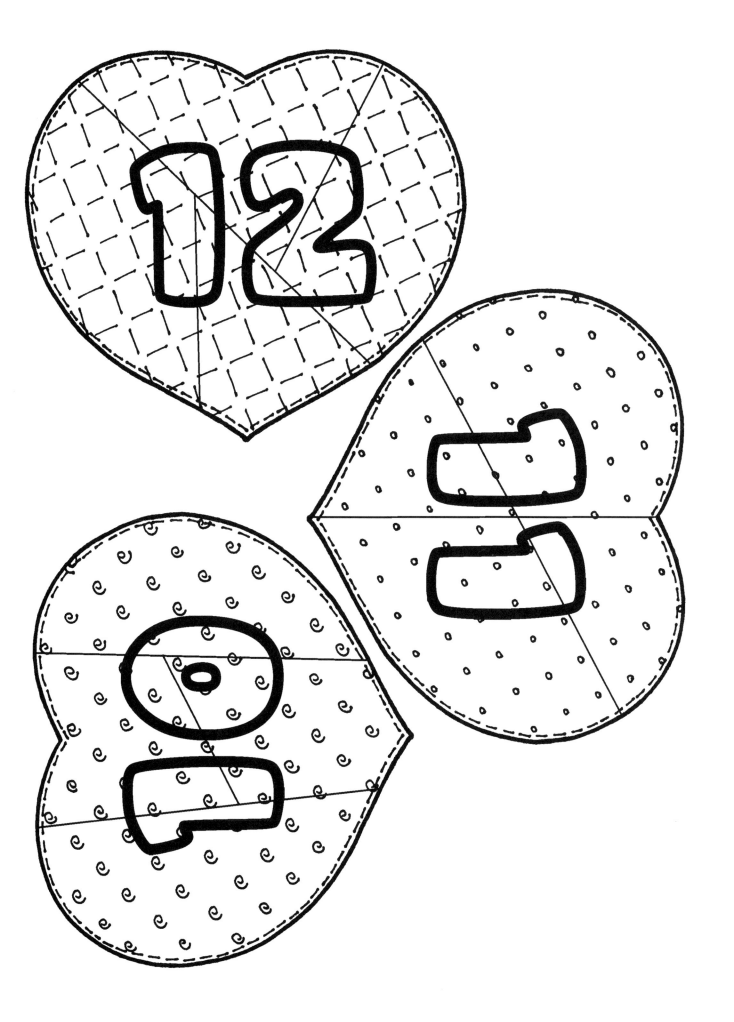

Cut carefully along the inside of the dotted line.

You're "Egg"stra Special Singers!

Do not cut along the dotted line. Use this margin to mount the other side.

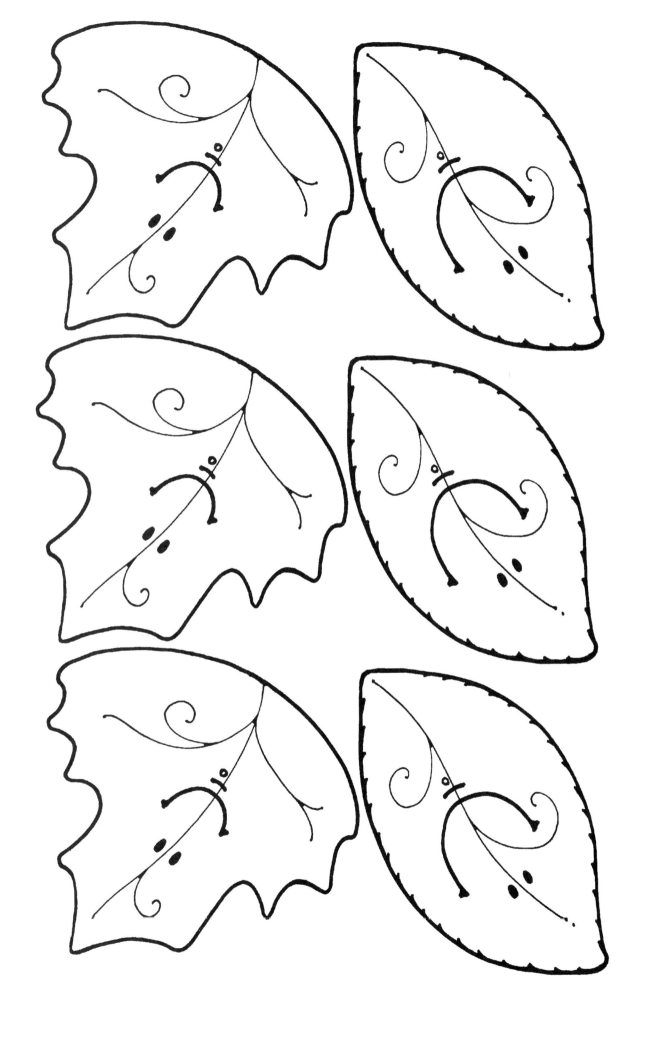

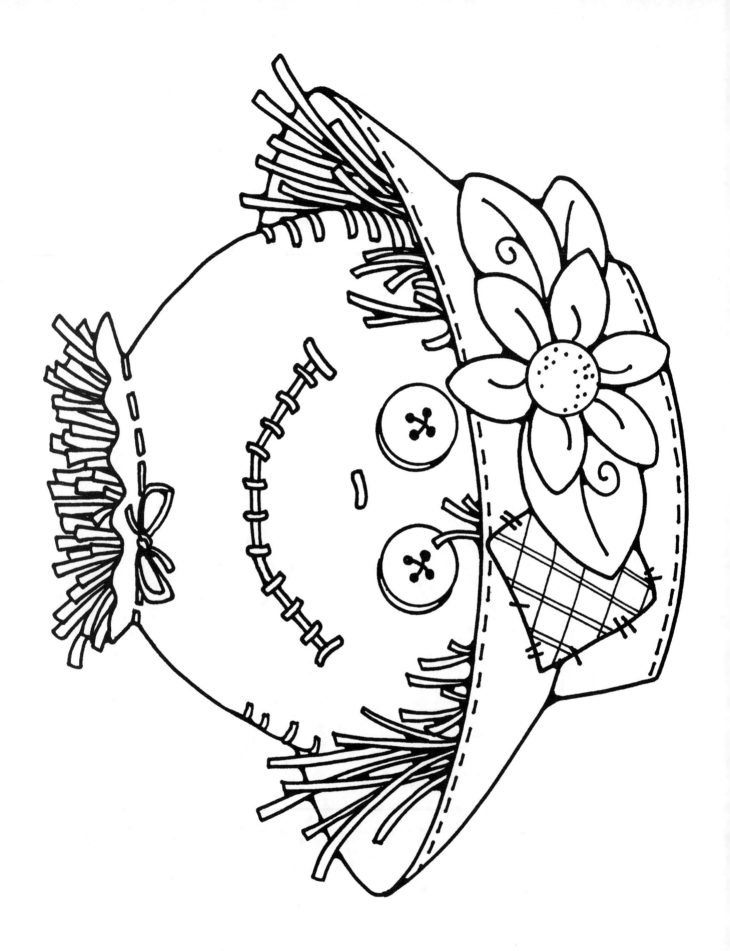

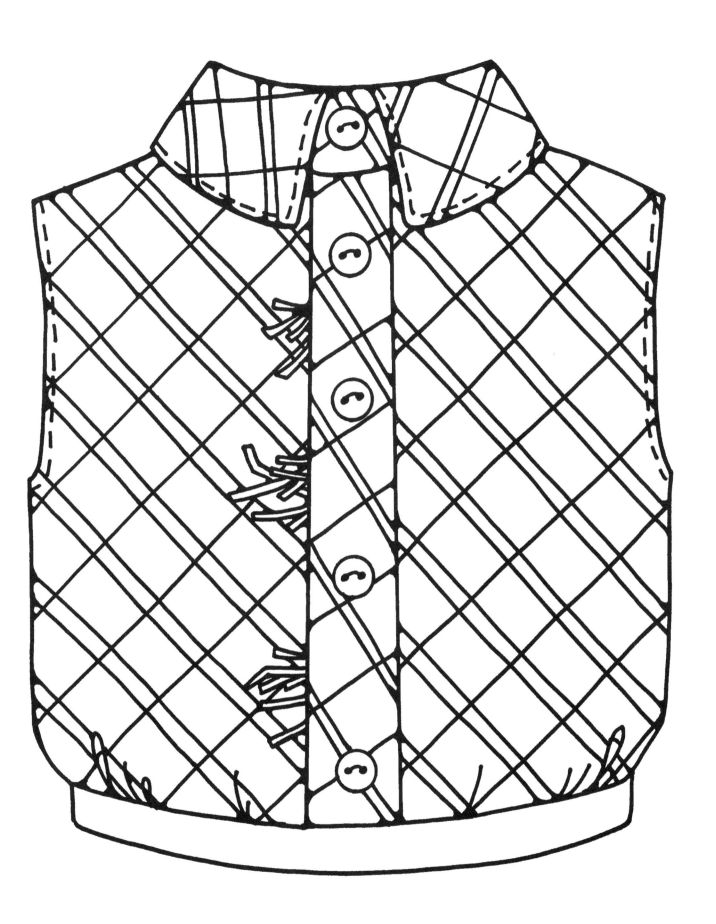

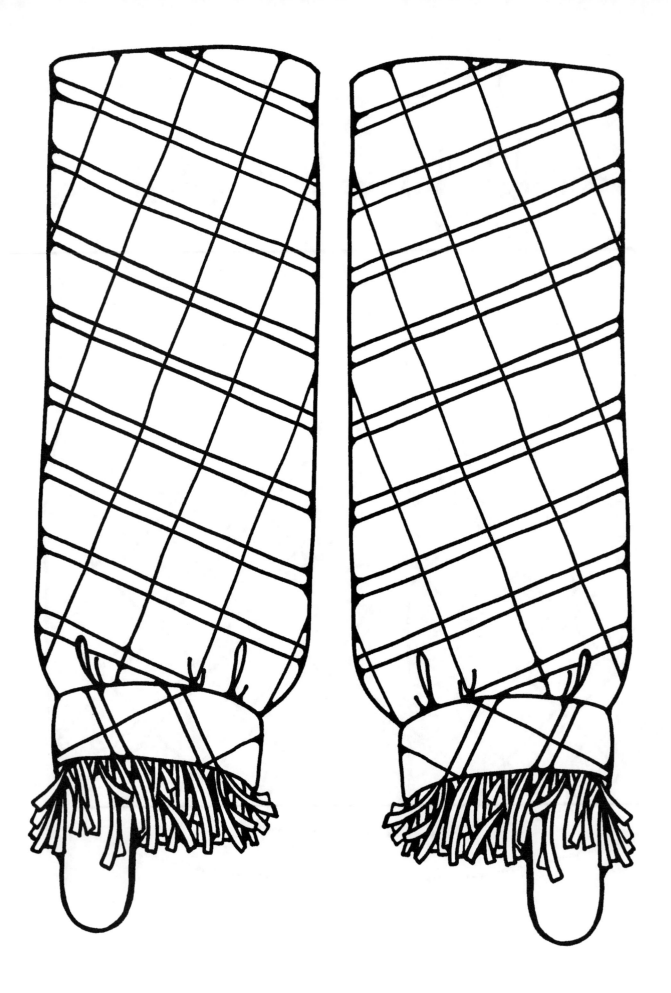

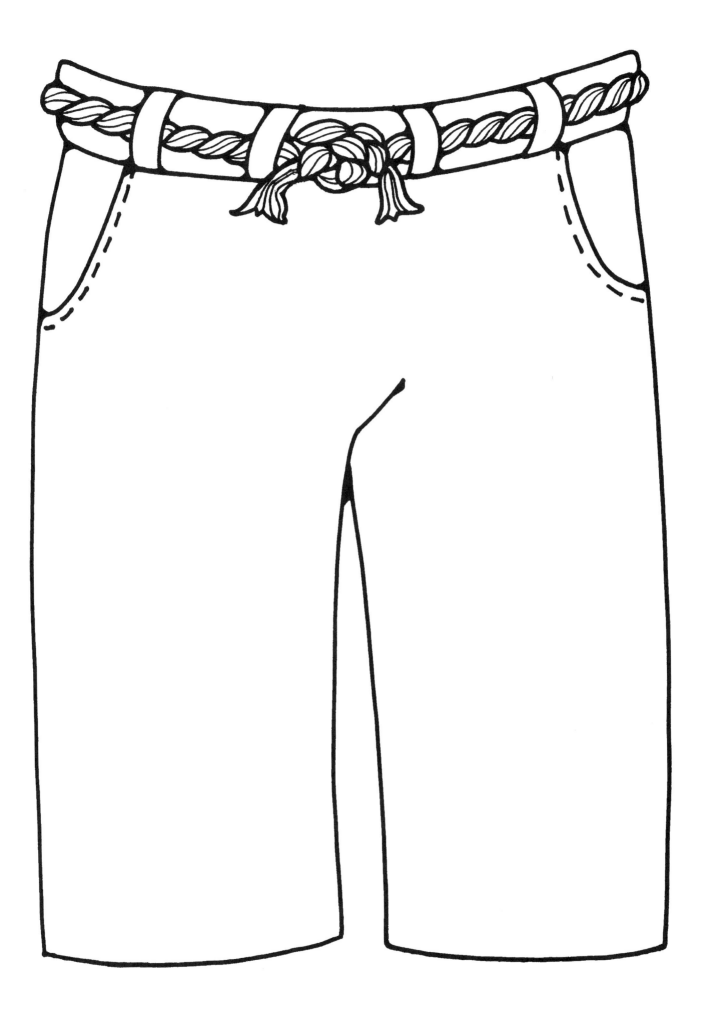

You're an "egg"stra special singer!

You're an "egg"stra special singer!

You're an "egg"stra special singer!

You're an "egg"stra special singer!

You're an "egg"stra special singer!

You're an "egg"stra special singer!

You're an "egg"stra special singer!

You're an "egg"stra special singer!

You're an "egg"stra special singer!

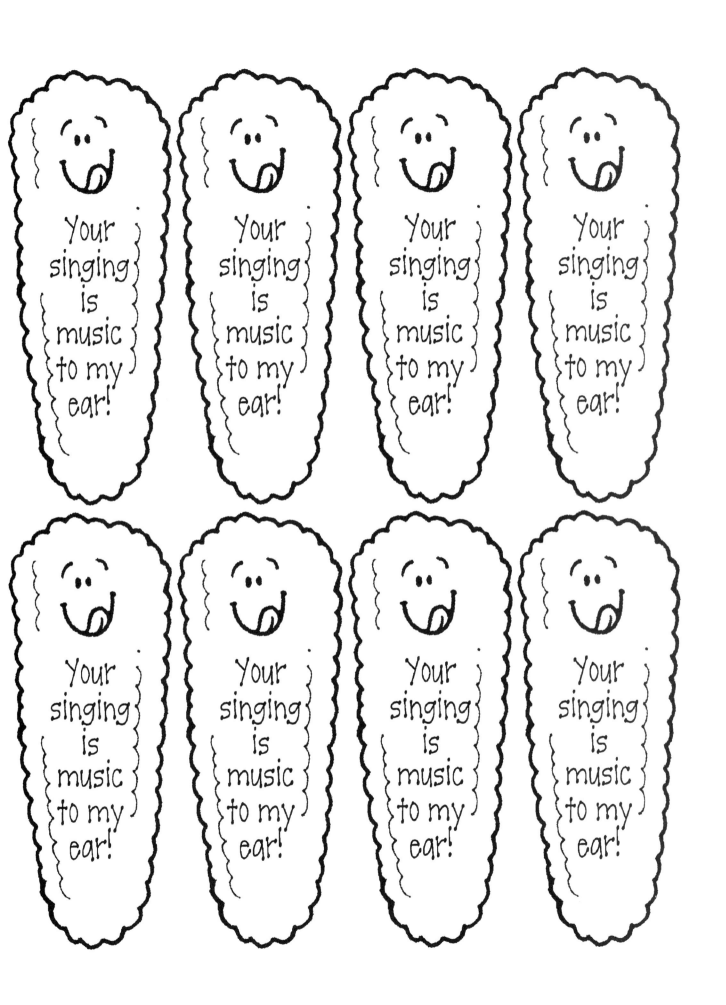

Enjoy More Singing Fun Motivators in Full-color, Ready-to-use:

Book 1: Super Singing Activities

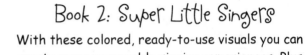

Book 2: Super Little Singers

With these colored, ready-to-use visuals you can create more memorable singing experiences. Plus, the visuals can be printed from the matching CD-ROM in color or black and white.

• In *Super Singing Activities* you'll find: Melody's Family Tree, Bird in the Leafy Treetops, Build a Snowman, Christmas Sing with Me, City of Enoch Singing Meter, Fill Noah's Ark Pick-a-song, and more.

• In *Super Little Singers* you'll find singing motivators, visuals and action activities for 28 songs (21 from the *Children's Songbook*). You'll love the visuals for seven all-time favorite children's songs, e.g., "Ants Go Marching," Eensy Weensy Spider," "Five Little Ducks," "Five Little Speckled Frogs," "Old MacDonald," "Twinkle, Twinkle, Little Star," and "Wheels on the Bus."